FROM CHALLENGE TO CHAMPION

INSPIRING STORIES OF BASEBALL GREATS

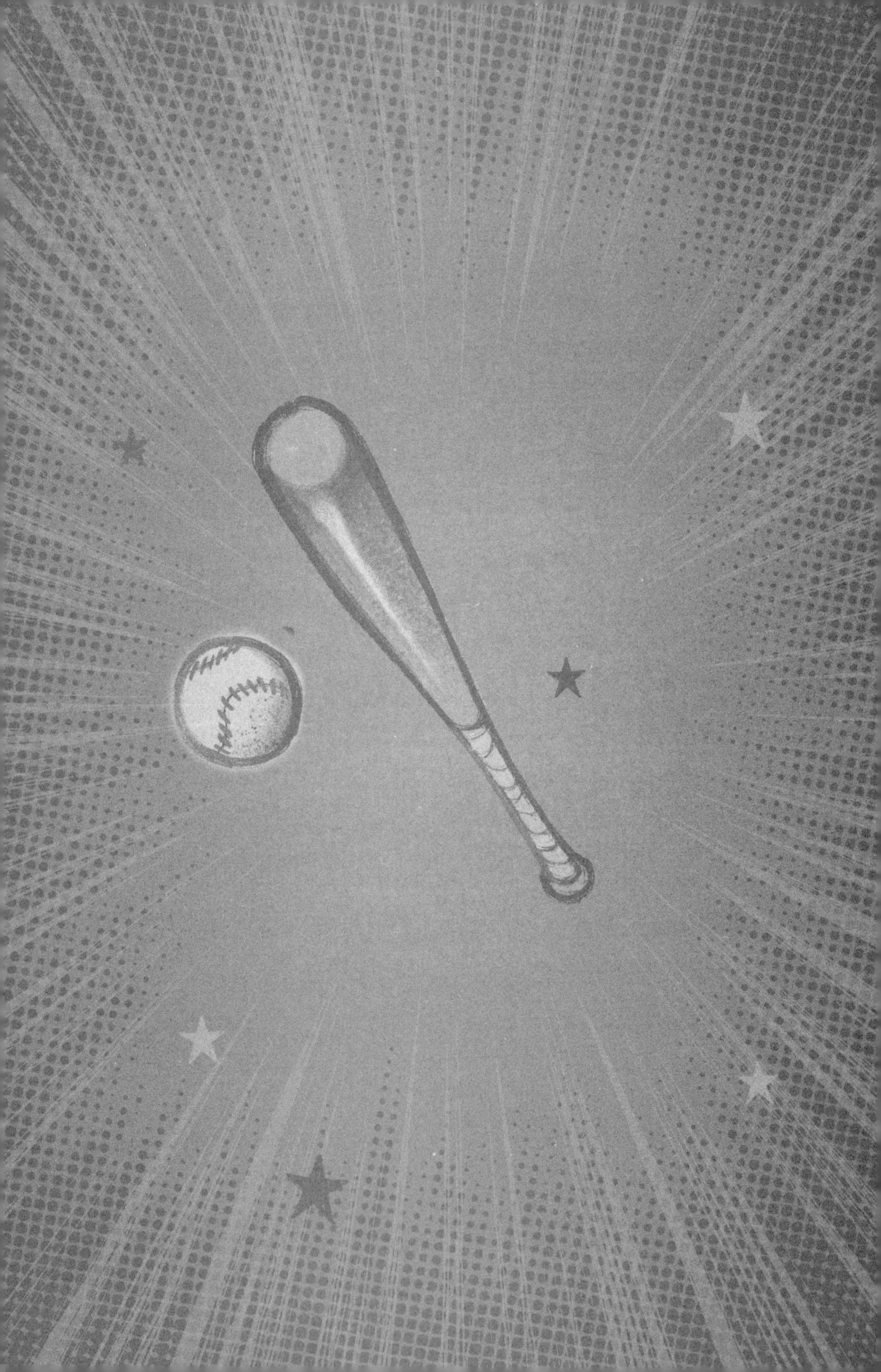

FROM CHALLENGE TO CHAMPION

INSPIRING STORIES OF BASEBALL GREATS

12 UPLIFTING TALES FOR KIDS

SKYLER TREPEL

Illustrated by Lorenzo Fornaciari

Z KIDS • NEW YORK

Z Kids
An imprint of Zeitgeist™
A division of Penguin Random House LLC
1745 Broadway, New York, NY 10019
zeitgeistpublishing.com
penguinrandomhouse.com

ISBN: 9798217151271
Ebook ISBN: 9798217151264

Printed in the United States of America
1st Printing

Illustrations by Lorenzo Fornaciari
Book design by Katy Brown
Author photograph © by Kayla Gordon
Illustrator photograph © by Jacopo Mastrangelo
Edited by Ada Fung

The authorized representative in the EU for product safety and compliance is Penguin Random House Ireland, Morrison Chambers, 32 Nassau Street, Dublin D02 YH68, Ireland. https://eu-contact.penguin.ie

To Nonna, the biggest baseball and Blue Jays fan I ever met, and my mom. Thank you both for teaching me to love reading, writing, and learning while supporting my dreams and teaching me many life lessons.

CONTENTS

HELLO, BASEBALL FANS!

The crack of the bat, the smell of hot dogs and peanuts, the roar of the crowd after a home run—these are just some of the things that make baseball so loved! Started in 1903, Major League Baseball (MLB) is the oldest professional sports league in the world. So, if you ask your grandma, grandpa, or even parents about baseball, they might have a story or two to tell you!

For me, Nonna (my grandma) is the person who gave me my love for baseball. She may have even been the biggest Toronto Blue Jays fan in the world! Even in her 70s, she watched every Blue Jays game and knew every statistic of every player. No matter what was going on in life, baseball made her happy as she yelled at the TV with joy and excitement. She loved reading and writing, too, and that's why I'm so excited to be writing this book about baseball dedicated to her and my mom.

Because baseball is such an old sport, this book features players like all-time great Babe Ruth, who began his career in 1914, and Jackie Robinson, who in 1947 was the first Black player to play in MLB. It also features more modern players like Derek Jeter, who won World Series titles in the late 1990s and 2000s, as well as some of today's biggest superstars, like Aaron Judge, Shohei Ohtani, Mookie Betts, and more.

These players may be stars, but they stood up for what they believed in, worked hard to overcome the challenges in their lives and careers, and never gave up on their dreams. In this book, you'll read all about the best stories in baseball history and learn lessons from these baseball stars that you can use to achieve your own dreams as you go from challenge to champion!

BASEBALL WORDS TO KNOW

Inning: A baseball game has nine innings. Each inning has a top (first) half and a bottom (second) half, where the teams switch who is playing offense and defense. When both teams have three outs, an inning ends. If the two teams are tied at the end of nine innings, they play extra innings until one team finishes an inning with more runs than the other.

Pitcher: The player who throws the ball to the batter, trying to strike them out.

Batter: A player on offense who hits the ball with a bat.

Fielder: A player on defense who tries to catch the ball after it's hit and tries to prevent the offense from scoring. In addition to the pitcher and catcher, there are four infielders and three outfielders.

Run: When a player reaches home plate, which adds one point to the team's score.

Home run: Sometimes called a "homer," this is when a ball is hit out of the baseball field, or when a batter is able to run all the bases before the ball reaches home plate.

Grand slam: When a player hits a home run with bases loaded (three runners on base), which counts for four runs.

RBI: When a player hits the ball and causes another runner to score a run, the hitter gets an RBI, or run(s) batted in.

Walk-off: A home run, grand slam, or RBI that ends the final inning and wins the game as the final play.

Stealing: This is when a player on base tries to quickly sneak to the next base without getting caught, even before the pitcher throws the ball.

Strike: A ball thrown within a space the batter can hit, called the strike zone, that the batter misses or doesn't swing at. Three strikes is called a strikeout, and the batter is out.

Ball: When the pitcher throws outside the strike zone and the batter doesn't swing.

Walk: If the pitcher throws four balls, the batter gets a walk to first base. Sometimes pitchers will throw balls on purpose if the batter is known for hitting home runs.

ERA: Earned run average (ERA) represents how many runs a pitcher gives up per game. A lower number means a better ERA, with 4.0 being considered good and 2.5 being considered amazing.

Batting percentage: A number determined by how many hits a player gets while batting, with .000 being the lowest and 1.000 being the highest. If a batter hits without getting out 3 out of 10 times batting, their batting average will be .300, which is considered an excellent average.

Error: When a fielder makes a mistake, such as dropping or missing a ball they could have easily caught or making a bad throw.

Foul ball: When a player hits a ball outside of the foul lines or poles of the baseball field. It counts as a strike, unless a player already has two strikes.

American League: Half of MLB's teams play in the American League (AL). The second round of the playoffs is the American League Division Series (ALDS), and the third round is the American League Championship Series (ALCS). The winner plays in the World Series.

National League: Half of MLB's teams play in the National League (NL). The second round of the playoffs is the National League Division Series (NLDS), and the third round is the National League Championship Series (NLCS). The winner plays in the World Series.

World Series: The final championship series between the winning teams of the ALCS and NLCS, in which the first team to win four out of seven possible games wins.

BABE RUTH

1

BABE RUTH

POSITION: Pitcher, right fielder

BIRTH DATE: February 6, 1895

HOMETOWN: Baltimore, Maryland

TEAMS: Boston Red Sox, New York Yankees, Boston Braves

BREAKOUT MOMENT: In 1916, Babe had the lowest (best) ERA in the league and hit three home runs and scored 18 runs to help the Boston Red Sox get to and win the World Series.

TOP ACHIEVEMENTS

- Seven-time World Series Champion
- 12-time American League home run leader
- 1923 American League MVP
- Member of the All-Time MLB Team
- Six-time American League RBI leader

DID YOU KNOW?

Although everyone knows Babe Ruth as “Babe,” his birth name is George Ruth.

He's considered the greatest baseball player of all time. Babe, also known as "the Great Bambino," was the all-time league leader in home runs when he retired. He had the most home runs in MLB for 11 seasons, which is still the record today! But he faced many struggles, both as a boy growing up and as a player. Babe might be known as the king of home runs, but he also had the most strikeouts. That shows that you've got to keep swinging no matter what—in life and baseball—if you want to succeed.

Babe was born over 125 years ago, and life was a lot different then. Babe's father worked at an old western bar all day and night, and his mother often suffered from poor health, so Babe was left alone a lot. He skipped school, wandered the streets, and got into trouble. Unable to handle him, Babe's parents sent him to a school for orphans and troubled children. The school was very strict, and there were lots of rules. It was hard for Babe to be sent away from home at first, but then something magical happened. He met a teacher, Brother Matthias, who became his mentor.

Brother Matthias loved baseball, and he taught Babe how to play. He helped Babe with his hitting, fielding, and pitching skills. In fact, he was like a father to Babe. As Babe said about Brother Matthias, "He taught me to read and write, and he taught me the difference between right and wrong. He was the father I needed and the greatest man I've ever known."

Babe was so good at baseball that the school invited Jack Dunn, the owner of the minor-league Baltimore Orioles, to watch Babe play. After less than an hour of watching, Jack offered Babe a contract. Because Babe was only 19 years old, Jack had to become his legal guardian before Babe could sign the contract. Without family support, Babe turned to Jack for help and guidance. Some players saw how close Jack and Babe were, so they started calling him "Jack's newest babe." This is how he became known as Babe Ruth.

In 1914, the Orioles minor-league team was losing money, so they had to sell Babe to the Boston Red Sox in MLB. Although Babe would become known for hitting many home runs—which was unusual in early baseball history—he was first known for his pitching ability. Since pitchers use their arm so much, they don't pitch every game. In his six seasons with the Red Sox, Babe won 89 games out of 139 games and had an impressive ERA of 2.19.

However, Babe wanted to bat, too, because he wanted to play in more games, and pitchers don't usually hit. Another player convinced the Red Sox manager to let Babe bat. Babe started hitting home runs immediately! In fact, he began hitting more home runs than anyone. But because he took such big swings, he also struck out a lot. Babe didn't let this stop him from batting. In fact, Babe said, "Every strike brings me closer to the next home run."

Babe won three World Series with the Red Sox. He was becoming known as one of

SOX

the best players in baseball for his rare ability to both hit and pitch. Most players could only pitch or hit, but Babe could do both almost better than anyone! While on the Red Sox, he even broke the record for most home runs in a season in 1919 with 29 runs.

After the 1919 season, Babe got traded to the New York Yankees because the Red Sox thought he was becoming too expensive. This shocked the baseball world at the time, since Babe was so popular and talented. Later, this trade became known as the "Curse of the Bambino," because the Red Sox didn't win a World Series for another 84 years after the Babe Ruth trade!

Maybe the Red Sox didn't believe Babe was worth the price anymore, but the Yankees did. Babe had already proved himself as one of the league's best pitchers, but he dreamed of hitting home runs. The Yankees let Babe become a full-time outfielder so he could bat every game. In his first season with the

Yankees, Babe broke his own record with 54 home runs. He broke his record again with 59 home runs the next year, and again in 1927 when he hit 60 home runs.

Babe was changing baseball from a low-scoring game with very few home runs to an exciting, high-scoring game. This transition became known as going from the "dead-ball era" to the "live-ball era." During his time with the Yankees, Babe helped lead them to the World Series seven times, winning the championship four of those times. He played with other great players like Earle Combs and Lou Gehrig. This era of the Yankees, from the 1920s to the 1930s, became one of the greatest dynasties in baseball history.

In the 1930s, the world was going through the Great Depression, and people had much less money than usual. Babe's incredible play on the field gave people hope and joy. Off the field, Babe made time for kids who were growing up in difficult circumstances like he did. He visited children's hospitals and orphanages and signed baseballs for young kids. Between his performance on the field and his generosity off the field, Babe is one of the most inspiring people in sports history.

Today, over 100 years after Babe played his first MLB game, people still talk about him regularly. Shohei Ohtani, the first player since Babe who can pitch and bat well, is often compared to Babe. But perhaps the best part of Babe's legacy is his belief that every strike only brings him closer to the next home run. That, dear readers, is the "from challenge to champion" mindset!

1947 BROOKLYN DODGERS

2

1947 BROOKLYN DODGERS

TEAM STARS

Jackie Robinson
first baseman

Branch Rickey
team president

Pee Wee Reese
shortstop

Dixie Walker
right fielder

Ralph Branca
pitcher

Bruce Edwards
catcher

Eddie Stanky
second baseman

TOP ACHIEVEMENTS

- 1947 National League champions
- 1947 World Series appearance
- Rookie of the Year Award (Jackie Robinson)

CLUTCH PLAYS

- On April 15, 1947, Jackie Robinson broke the color barrier—and scored an important run in the Dodgers' win.
- The Dodgers finished first in the National League, becoming the first racially integrated team to play in the World Series.

The 1947 Brooklyn Dodgers are considered baseball's most important team. Why? On April 15, opening day of the 1947 season, Jackie Robinson broke baseball's color barrier. He became the first Black player in MLB since non-white players were banned over 50 years before Jackie started playing, and before the World Series even existed. To mark this historic day, MLB celebrates Jackie Robinson Day every year on April 15, and every major-league player wears uniform number 42 in his honor.

Breaking the color barrier took a lot of courage from Robinson. However, he would not have had this opportunity to make history without team president Branch Rickey. In 1903, as the coach of Ohio Wesleyan University's baseball team, Rickey tried to check his team into a hotel. But the hotel tried to stop the team's catcher, Charles Thomas, from staying there because he was Black.

Many years later, this injustice inspired Rickey to find the right player to bring up from the Negro Leagues, a league for Black players. ("Negro" is not an appropriate word today, but it is used when talking about baseball's history so people can learn from it and avoid making the same mistakes.) Rickey also recognized that there were many Black fans who would love to see a Black player. As a businessman, he knew this would bring more great players and a wider fan base to baseball.

In 1945, Robinson was playing for the Kansas City Monarchs in the Negro Leagues. He and his team faced a lot of racism. They were not allowed to use bathrooms at some places and had trouble finding hotels to stay in. All the difficulty Robinson faced was part of what made Rickey think Robinson was the right player to break the color barrier.

When Rickey called Robinson to ask him to join the Dodgers, he warned Robinson that many people would not be happy to see a Black player in MLB. But Rickey believed Robinson would have "guts enough not to fight back." If Robinson could stay calm and not react to the racism he would surely face, he would have the chance to become a great baseball player. He'd also open the doors for other non-white players to play in MLB.

Not every Dodger wanted Robinson to join the team. Some players even signed a petition, led by outfielder Dixie Walker, against letting him play. Others, including the team manager, thought Robinson should be given a chance. One player who refused to sign the petition was shortstop Pee Wee Reese, who would become Robinson's close friend. The manager called a meeting and told the team that no matter what Robinson looked like, he deserved to play baseball and be a part of the Dodgers. Walker and the other players would simply have to learn to play with, and accept, Robinson.

On opening day, just as Rickey had predicted, Robinson drew a crowd, half of whom were Black, leading to many cheers for

him. Although there were still boos, history was made, and the Dodgers won—with Robinson scoring an important run late in the game!

Although the Dodgers were winning games, Robinson wasn't playing well at first. Even though some of his own teammates thought he should be benched (removed from the starting lineup), Robinson stayed in the lineup and got better. But the racism and hateful comments didn't stop. In Philadelphia,

Phillies manager Ben Chapman shouted racist comments toward Robinson, encouraging his players to do the same. Robinson kept his cool, but his teammate Eddie Stanky couldn't stand it. He told Chapman to stop. Eventually, other Dodgers players stood up to Chapman, too. It was a tough day, but it ended up bringing the team closer together.

Unfortunately, Robinson continued getting insulted wherever he went. In Cincinnati, the fans were booing Robinson and yelling horrible things at him. Reese walked over and put his arm around Robinson. Reese was the captain of the team, and his gesture signaled to the fans and players to show Robinson respect. This wasn't just another moment that brought the Dodgers closer together. Many sports historians consider this the point when most fans stopped booing Robinson and started to accept non-white players in MLB.

Off the field, the Dodgers were coming together, too. Players head to the showers at

the same time after games. At the start of the season, Robinson would wait because he knew that many of his teammates didn't want him there. One day, pitcher Ralph Branca invited Robinson to the showers with the rest of the team, and most players accepted him.

The closeness of the team helped them play great baseball. They were known for playing a smart game focused on speed, pitching, and defense. Robinson won Rookie of the Year and helped the Dodgers lead the league in stolen bases. Branca, Walker, Reese, Stanky, and catcher Bruce Edwards were selected to play in the All-Star Game.

The Dodgers finished first in the National League, becoming the first racially integrated team to play in the World Series. This was also the first World Series shown on TV! The Dodgers won three games out of six to take the series to Game 7 before losing to the New York Yankees. The Dodgers may not have won the championship, but they proved that you don't need to win a championship to be champions. They are champions for how they changed baseball.

Because of Robinson and the Dodgers, over 40 percent of baseball players today come from diverse backgrounds. Robinson deserves all the credit for the abuse he put up with to fight against racism in baseball. However, he couldn't have done this without Rickey's belief in him and his teammates' support. They changed Robinson's life, which helped him impact the lives of millions. As Robinson has said, "A life is not important except in the impact it has on other lives."

DID YOU KNOW?

The 1947 Brooklyn Dodgers season was turned into a movie called *42*, featuring *Black Panther* star Chadwick Boseman as Jackie Robinson and *Star Wars* star Harrison Ford as Branch Rickey.

HANK AARON

3

HANK AARON

POSITION: Right fielder

BIRTH DATE: February 5, 1934

HOMETOWN: Mobile, Alabama

TEAMS: Milwaukee/Atlanta Braves, Milwaukee Brewers

BREAKOUT MOMENT: In 1957, Hank won the National League MVP while leading the league in home runs and RBIs as he led the Braves to a World Series win.

TOP ACHIEVEMENTS

- 25-time All-Star
- World Series champion
- 1957 National League MVP
- Four-time National League home run leader
- Three-time Gold Glove Award winner

DID YOU KNOW?

Hank Aaron was awarded the Presidential Medal of Freedom in 2002 for both his baseball career and civil rights activism.

Hank Aaron is one of the best hitters in baseball history. He was named an All-Star a record 25 times and became the all-time home run leader. In fact, MLB's award for the best offensive player in the National and American Leagues is named after him! However, growing up, Hank didn't even have enough money to hit an actual baseball, which makes his journey that much more impressive.

Hank was born in Mobile, Alabama, as the third of eight kids. His parents worked hard to support their large family, and they didn't have much money. Hank loved baseball, and he may not have had the money for a ball and a bat, but this didn't stop him from playing. Instead, Hank used a stick as a bat and a bottle cap as a ball. He was determined to do whatever it took to achieve his dreams of playing professional baseball.

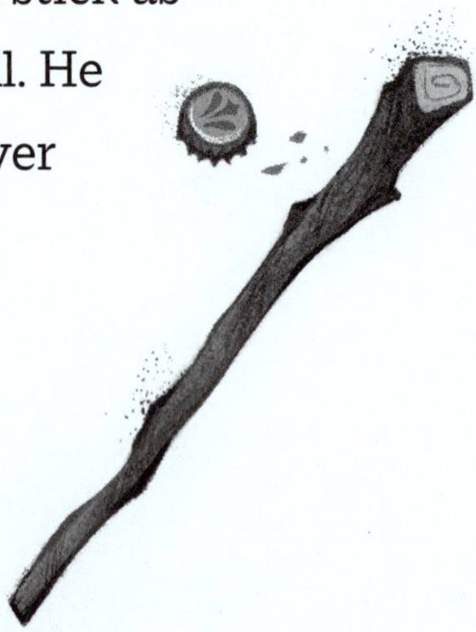

Having no money wasn't the only challenge that Hank had to face. He also lived in a segregated town, meaning that Black people had to live in a different neighborhood than white people. This was unfortunately common in America at the time. Hank faced a lot of racism growing up, and baseball helped him find joy and escape the terrible things going on around him.

Hank knew that being Black meant he had less of a chance to play in MLB. Jackie Robinson had broken the color barrier in 1947, when Hank was 13. But change was slow, and it took time for Black players to be fully accepted into MLB. So Hank began his career playing in the Negro Leagues when he was 18.

The next year, the Milwaukee Braves purchased Hank's contract and had him play for their minor-league teams. Hank wasn't allowed to stay in the same hotel rooms as his teammates, or even change in the same locker rooms, because he was Black. This was very tough on him, but he knew that continuing to play would help other Black players. He also didn't want to give up on his dreams. As Hank said, "My motto was always to keep swinging. Whether I was in a slump or feeling badly or having trouble off the field, the only thing to do was keep swinging."

In 1954, Hank's hard work paid off, and he got called up to play with the Milwaukee Braves in MLB. Because the color barrier had been broken so recently, Hank knew he would have to work extra hard to prove he belonged in MLB. Hank didn't hit his first home run until his seventh game, but once he got going, he couldn't be stopped!

Hank made his first All-Star appearances in 1955 and 1956, but in 1957, he really showed the world he was the next big thing in baseball. That year, he won the National League MVP Award while leading the league in both home runs and RBIs. He finished with an incredible .322 batting average, 44 home runs, and 132

RBIs in the regular season. But he wasn't done yet. To win the National League and take the Braves to the World Series, Hank hit a game-winning walk-off two-run homer (home run) in the 11th inning. He skipped around the bases, celebrating with his teammates in a moment he'd always dreamed about.

In the World Series, Hank was the star of the show, with an amazing .393 batting average, three home runs, and seven RBIs, leading all hitters in those categories. The Braves went on to win the World Series, with Hank celebrated as the best player on the team.

Hank brought his own brand of swing to the plate, waiting until the last second and swinging quickly at the ball. But Hank was really consistent. He made the All-Star Game every year from 1955 to 1975, hit 30 home runs in 15 separate seasons, and batted over .300 in 14 seasons. Hank's consistency led him to an incredible achievement: At the end of the

1973 season, Hank had 713 career home runs. This meant that he was about to break Babe Ruth's home run record of 714 at the start of the next season.

Not everyone was happy about this. There were still racist fans who didn't want a Black man to have what many consider baseball's most important individual record. Hank received nearly a million letters from fans insulting him and making racist comments about why they didn't want him to break the record. This hurt Hank a lot, but once again, he would not let other people stop him from pursuing his dreams.

On opening day of the 1974 season, Hank swung hard, like he always did, and tied Babe Ruth's all-time home run record. A few days later, during the Braves' first home game of the season, "Hammerin' Hank," as he was known, hammered the ball into left-center field. Home run! Hank had broken a record that once felt unbreakable!

Braves
44

Despite all the hate Hank had received, he brought an entire stadium together as everyone stood and cheered for him.

Hank retired in 1976 with 755 home runs as the new all-time home run leader. His record was eventually broken by Barry Bonds, but, as of 2025, Hank still holds the record for most RBIs with 2,297 and most total bases with 6,856.

Hank didn't just come a long way from his own humble beginnings; he also helped baseball come a long way from its racist beginnings. In large part because of Hank's greatness and determination, fans learned to cheer on and celebrate players, no matter the color of their skin.

Hank's experiences with racism in baseball inspired him to become a civil rights activist. He supported civil rights organizations like the National Association for the Advancement of Colored People (NAACP). He and his wife founded the Hank Aaron Chasing the Dream

Foundation, which gives scholarships to underprivileged youth to help them chase their dreams.

In 2002, he was awarded the Presidential Medal of Freedom for his work as a civil rights hero. As Hank said, "I think that people can look at me and say, 'He was a great baseball player, but he was even a greater human being.'"

ROBERTO CLEMENTE

4

ROBERTO CLEMENTE

POSITION: Right fielder

BIRTH DATE: August 18, 1934

HOMETOWN: Carolina, Puerto Rico

TEAM: Pittsburgh Pirates

BREAKOUT MOMENT: In 1960, Roberto made his first All-Star Game and helped lead the Pittsburgh Pirates to a World Series championship.

TOP ACHIEVEMENTS

- Two-time World Series champion
- 15-time All-Star
- 12-time Gold Glove Award winner
- 1966 National League MVP
- 1971 World Series MVP

DID YOU KNOW?

In 2002, MLB officially named September 15 Roberto Clemente Day.

Every year since 1973, the Roberto Clemente Award is given to an MLB player who best represents excellence in baseball, sportsmanship, and community involvement. This award perfectly represents Roberto Clemente. He wasn't just an amazing baseball player on the field; he was also dedicated to helping others off the field.

Born in Puerto Rico, Roberto was the youngest of seven children. His father didn't make much money working as a sugarcane crop supervisor, so as a boy Roberto started working with his dad to help his family. He helped his dad put shovels into construction trucks and did other jobs for neighbors to make money. Life wasn't always easy for Roberto, but one thing that got him through it was his love of baseball.

As a kid, Roberto loved going to watch games in the Puerto Rico Winter Baseball League, a league that would one day be named after him. Roberto didn't have enough money to get into the stadium, so he would climb a tree to watch the games. It was still a time when non-white players weren't allowed to play in MLB, so he especially enjoyed watching Monte Irvin, a Black player from the Negro Leagues who played in Puerto Rico in the offseason.

When Roberto was 11 years old, he saw Monte outside the stadium. He walked up to Monte and told him how much he admired him. Monte gave Roberto his bag so Roberto could walk into the stadium for free. Once inside, he gave Roberto a baseball glove. This act of kindness changed Roberto's life. Seeing a kind person who looked like him play professional baseball inspired Roberto to believe that he, too, could play professional baseball.

Roberto was very athletic. In high school, he ran track and was a star javelin thrower. But his dream was still to play professional baseball. He played in Puerto Rico's amateur baseball league and joined the Puerto Rican Professional Baseball League when he was just 18 years old. Pretty soon, his arm strength and .288 batting average caught the interest of MLB's Brooklyn Dodgers. They signed him to their minor-league team. He didn't get a lot of playing time, but the Pittsburgh Pirates liked what they saw and signed him the next season. Roberto's dream had come true!

But his start in MLB had its challenges. Although Jackie Robinson had broken the color barrier almost 10 years earlier, there was still a lot of racism in baseball. Roberto was part of the first wave of Latino players in MLB, he was Black, and his first language was Spanish, not English. Some journalists would misspell words on purpose when they reported what Roberto said, like writing "heet" when he said “hit,” making fun of his accent. Roberto felt disrespected, but he knew if he focused on baseball, he could do great things and pave the way for other Latino and Hispanic players.

Roberto had a quick, strong throwing arm, which allowed him to get players out with ease. He was also a powerful batter. He was amazing at getting RBIs, which was especially clear during a 1956 game. The Pirates were down by three in the ninth inning, and Roberto hit a walk-off grand slam to win the game!

In 1958, Roberto hit three triples (a hit that got him on third base) in one game to help lead the Pirates to victory. In 1960, he had a .314 batting average, recorded 94 RBIs, and helped the Pirates win the World Series. But even with all his talent, many people still didn’t know who Roberto was. He played in Pittsburgh, where players didn’t get as much media attention as players in big cities like New York and Los Angeles.

But before long, people couldn't deny how great Roberto was. He won 12 Gold Glove Awards in a row, tying the record for the most won by an outfielder. He became a 15-time All-Star. In 1966, Roberto finally got national recognition as the National League MVP.

Roberto's greatness would shine brightest in the 1971 World Series against the Baltimore Orioles. It didn't start well for Roberto and the Pirates—they lost the first two games. But Roberto batted an outstanding .414 average in that series. In Game 6, he caught a ball near the back of the field and made an incredible throw to home plate to get an important out. But Roberto's best play of the series? A solo home run to help Pittsburgh win Game 7 in a comeback victory! Roberto was the first Latino named World Series MVP. A year later, Roberto became the 11th player—and the first Latino—to bat 3,000 career hits.

Roberto wasn't just one of baseball's all-time great players; he was also an

extraordinary and generous person. Just like Monte was to him, Roberto was especially kind to young kids. He stayed long after games to sign autographs and chat with kids who looked up to him. He hosted baseball clinics for kids so they could learn the sport, make connections, and pursue their own dreams. He also sent money and supplies to Latin American countries, including his island home of Puerto Rico.

In December 1972, an earthquake hit Managua, Nicaragua. It caused lots of damage and left many people without water, food, and medicine. Roberto raised $150,000—worth over $1 million today—to help the people of Nicaragua. But the first few shipments of supplies were never delivered. So on New Year's Eve, Roberto took a plane full of supplies to deliver to Nicaragua. Sadly, the plane crashed, and Roberto passed away. After his passing, Roberto was inducted into the National Baseball Hall of Fame and Pirates Hall of Fame.

Out of this tragedy came a beautiful, positive legacy. Roberto has inspired Latino and Hispanic players all over the world to play baseball. But his legacy, just like his life, goes beyond the baseball field. MLB named their humanitarian award after Roberto, and as part of that award, MLB donates money to a charity of the winner's choice. Roberto's family continues to help people through the Roberto

Clemente Foundation, which promotes "positive change and community engagement through the example and inspiration of Roberto."

REGGIE JACKSON

5

REGGIE JACKSON

POSITION: Right fielder

BIRTH DATE: May 18, 1946

HOMETOWN: Wyncote, Pennsylvania

TEAMS: Kansas City/Oakland Athletics, Baltimore Orioles, New York Yankees, California Angels

BREAKOUT MOMENT: In 1969, Reggie made his first All-Star team after hitting a career-high 47 home runs.

TOP ACHIEVEMENTS

- Five-time World Series champion
- Two-time World Series MVP
- 14-time All-Star
- Four-time American League home run leader

DID YOU KNOW?

Reggie hosted his own kids' sports show, *Reggie Jackson's World of Sports*, on Nickelodeon and has played himself in many movies and TV shows.

Reggie Jackson has one of the best nicknames in baseball: "Mr. October." This is because Reggie played at his best in the World Series, which usually happens in October. He has won five World Series titles and was named World Series MVP twice. Reggie overcame many challenges along the way, which helped him play well under pressure.

Reggie's childhood wasn't easy, because of the racism he faced. He loved watching baseball but had to sit in a designated "colored" section for people who weren't white. Reggie's family was one of the only Black families in his hometown of Wyncote, Pennsylvania. Sports helped him bond with other kids, but Reggie still experienced racism.

Once, Reggie's friend lent him a bike so that Reggie wouldn't have to walk home. Reggie was halfway home when his friend's stepfather saw Reggie on the bike. He made Reggie take it all the way back to their place just because Reggie was Black.

Reggie's dad told him that the best way to deal with being treated badly was by working hard to be even better than everyone else. Reggie took this advice, and became good enough at baseball to play with the Birmingham A's in the minor leagues.

But because he was Black, Reggie had a hard time finding a place to live. Some of his teammates let him stay at their apartment, but when other people found out Reggie was there, they threatened to burn the building down. Reggie had to move into a hotel.

Reggie continues to talk about these hurtful, racist experiences today because, as he said, "There's times when you need to bring up these painful things that you've lived with. There's times to let those out because the stories that we have to tell about baseball, baseball would rather us forget."

After he joined MLB's Kansas City Athletics, Reggie still faced racism, but his father's advice and support from his teammates helped Reggie focus on baseball. During his third season, in 1969, with the team now playing in Oakland, California, Reggie scored a career-high 47 home runs and got over 100 runs and over 100 RBIs!

Reggie had proved how amazing he was, but he wasn't being paid fairly. He said he wouldn't play until he got paid what he was worth. The owner threatened to send him to the minor leagues if he didn't play. Reggie wanted to stay in MLB, so he played, but when he had a brief slump, the owner benched him.

During one game, Reggie was finally called on to play. He was angry about being benched, but he knew he had to play his best and show how good he could be. Reggie swung as hard as he could and smacked a game-winning home run to center field for a grand slam, winning the game. This was how Reggie stood up for himself—by proving he was too good to stay benched.

In 1972, Reggie played a big part in the Athletics' postseason. In the game that would decide whether the team made it to the World Series, Reggie got a walk to first base, stole second base, dove head-first into third, and stole home base for a run to help them win. Unfortunately for Reggie, he injured his left leg and had to sit out the World Series. The Athletics won, but sitting out was hard for Reggie. It motivated him to come back better than ever, which he did.

In 1973, Reggie had his best year yet. He led the American League in RBIs and was named the league MVP. In the World Series,

he had six RBIs, batted .310, scored three runs, and hit a home run to help the Athletics win again. Reggie was named World Series MVP!

In 1974, Reggie helped lead the Athletics to their third World Series win in a row. By this point, he was one of the most famous baseball stars in the world. He was known for his outgoing personality—and for being the first baseball player to have a mustache and beard!

In 1975, Reggie led the league in home runs. But the Athletics' owner cut Reggie's pay, saying that Reggie struck out too much (even though this is part of hitting so many home runs). Reggie felt this was unfair and asked for a trade, so the owner traded him to the Baltimore Orioles. At the end of the season, he left Baltimore and signed a five-year contract with the New York Yankees for nearly $3 million—the biggest contract in baseball at the time.

If Reggie was a star before, now he was a *superstar*, playing for the most famous and successful franchise in MLB history. He was openly confident in himself and his talent. However, this rubbed some players and the manager, Billy Martin, the wrong way. They felt like Reggie was acting as if he was better than the rest of the team. Not being liked by people on his own team was tough, and Reggie struggled with his batting the first few months. Fans even began to boo Reggie for not getting along with Billy.

Yankees owner George Steinbrenner stepped in and asked Billy to let Reggie bat fourth in the lineup, known as the "cleanup" batter—the role that Reggie was most comfortable with. Reggie's batting improved, and so did his relationship with Billy. The two of them coming together united the Yankees, and they made it to the 1977 World Series.

In October 1977, the Dodgers were up 3–2 on the Yankees in Game 6 of the World Series. Reggie batted three times and hit three home runs, tying Babe Ruth's record for home runs

NY

in a World Series game. With five total home runs in the World Series—which the Yankees won—Reggie earned himself the nickname "Mr. October."

Reggie won the World Series again in 1978 and played for almost 10 more seasons. Since he retired from playing, Reggie has spoken up about getting more minorities in baseball. Reggie does interviews and shows, talking about the racism he faced in baseball and the need for more diversity and inclusion in baseball. Nearly 40 years after retiring, Mr. October is still changing the game and making an impact as a baseball legend.

JIM ABBOTT

6

JIM ABBOTT

POSITION: Pitcher

BIRTH DATE: September 19, 1967

HOMETOWN: Flint, Michigan

TEAMS: California Angels, New York Yankees, Chicago White Sox, Milwaukee Brewers

BREAKOUT MOMENT: On September 4, 1993, Jim pitched a no-hitter despite having only been born with one hand.

TOP ACHIEVEMENTS

- 1987 Golden Spikes Award
- 1988 Olympic Gold medalist
- 1988 Big Ten Conference Player of the Year
- Tony Conigliaro Award

DID YOU KNOW?

In 1993, Jim guest-starred as himself on the popular show *Boy Meets World* to teach the main character Cory Matthews about the value of getting an education while chasing your dreams.

Jim Abbott was born with only one hand. Twenty-five years later, Jim pitched a no-hitter in MLB, meaning no one got a hit off his pitches. It became one of the most inspirational stories in sports history. But how did someone with one hand even *make* MLB? By not letting his physical difference define him and never giving up!

On his first day of kindergarten, Jim showed up wearing a mechanical hand in place of his right hand. But it didn't feel right. Eventually, Jim got rid of the mechanical hand and let everyone see his arm, even if it looked different.

Jim's parents encouraged him to focus on what he did have, instead of what he didn't have. What Jim had was a love for sports. He wanted to fit in with other kids, and playing sports became a way for him to do so. Jim's parents thought soccer would be easier, because it doesn't require your hands. But Jim loved baseball, and it turned out that Jim was great at pitching! In fact, he pitched a no-hitter in his first Little League game! But how would he play defense and catch?

Jim worked hard by himself. He would bounce a rubber ball off a wall and practice catching it. He learned how to catch the ball with his gloved left hand, use his right arm to quickly take the glove off, and balance the glove on his right arm while throwing the ball with his left hand. He would then quickly put the glove back on his left hand to catch it again.

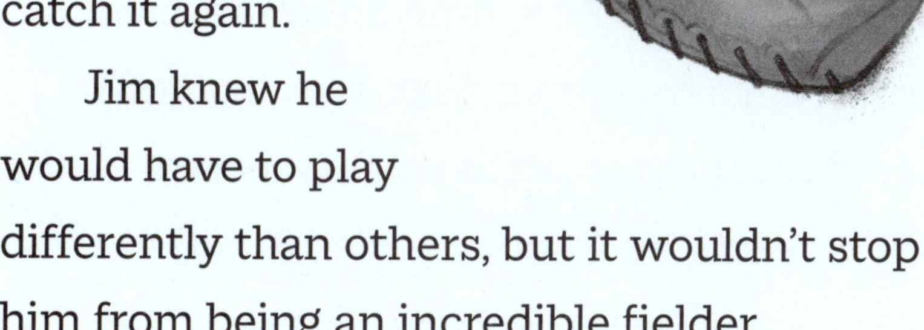

Jim knew he would have to play differently than others, but it wouldn't stop him from being an incredible fielder.

In his senior year of high school, Jim batted .427, hit seven home runs, and had an incredible ERA of .76. He also played first base when he wasn't pitching, showcasing his fielding skills and glove-switching ability he'd worked so hard on.

But even with his impressive play, Jim's high school coach said he'd never play in MLB and that he should go to college instead. Jim refused to let his coach decide his future, but he did think college would help him get an education *and* get better at baseball. So, even though he was drafted by the Toronto Blue Jays straight out of high school, Jim went to the University of Michigan.

People weren't sure Jim would succeed in college baseball. Once again, Jim proved the doubters wrong, earning an impressive 6–2 record his freshman year. He did even better the next year, with an 11–3 record, which earned him a spot on the United States national team. In 1987, Jim won the Golden Spikes Award, given by MLB to the best amateur baseball player. In 1988, he was named the Big Ten Conference Player of the

Year and helped lead the United States to an Olympic gold medal in baseball!

That same year, Jim was drafted eighth overall to the California Angels. During spring training, Jim did so well that he skipped the minor leagues and went straight to the majors. He was only the 15th player ever to do so! With 12 wins as the starting pitcher in his rookie year, Jim had the most wins by a rookie in nearly 100 years.

After a great first year, Jim experienced some ups and downs in his career. But as always, he kept working to improve. In 1991, Jim had one of his best seasons and placed third in voting for the Cy Young Award, given to the best pitcher in baseball. That year, he posted a 2.89 ERA—the fourth best in the American League—and got 18 wins as the starting pitcher. In 1992, Jim won only 7 games, but he posted an even better ERA of 2.77. He also won the Tony Conigliaro Award, given to MLB player who best overcomes challenges.

In the offseason, the Angels traded Jim to the New York Yankees. At first, Jim's play wasn't consistent. Because the Yankees were so famous, Jim had even more pressure and media attention on him. Some fans complained that he couldn't pitch as well because he had only one hand.

Jim wouldn't let his doubters define him. He got better, even almost pitching a no-hitter. He made it through eight innings—nearly the whole game—before giving up a hit. Pitching a no-hitter is extremely rare for any pitcher, let alone someone with one hand! But that was just a taste of things to come.

On September 4, 1993, Jim made baseball history. At the beginning of the game, Jim threw some pitches that weren't great, walking some players to first base. However, by the fifth inning, Jim realized he was halfway through the game and still hadn't thrown a hit. Fans realized this, too. The whole crowd cheered him on, knowing they were seeing something special.

25

By the final inning, fans were standing up and cheering for Jim at every pitch. How did Jim deal with the pressure? He focused on one pitch at a time, which helped him throw his best fastballs yet. Jim had already gotten two batters out. He only needed to get one more batter out. And that's just what he did. Jim threw a no-hitter in Yankee Stadium, baseball's most historic stadium!

Jim retired in 1999 and became a motivational speaker, continuing to inspire people born with physical differences. He wrote a book about his life, *Imperfect: An Improbable Life*. The title sums up Jim's journey well. He may not be perfect (nobody is!), but he never let his differences and challenges stop him from achieving his dreams.

As Jim said, "Imagine if we could look at misfortune and challenge and adversity as if it was a gift. As if it was a chance to reveal inner strength, as if we could embrace those challenges that come at us. [. . .] I hope you all know that nothing can stop you if you can be tough, if you can be creative, if you can believe in who you are and what you can do. Nothing in this world can hold you back."

DEREK JETER

7

DEREK JETER

POSITION: Shortstop

BIRTH DATE: June 26, 1974

HOMETOWNS: Pequannock Township, New Jersey; Kalamazoo, Michigan

TEAM: New York Yankees

BREAKOUT MOMENT: In 1996, Derek was named the American League Rookie of the Year as the Yankees' starting shortstop and helped lead them to a World Series title.

TOP ACHIEVEMENTS

- 2014 Commissioner's Historic Achievement Award
- Five-time World Series champion
- 2000 World Series MVP
- 14-time All-Star
- 1996 American League Rookie of the Year

DID YOU KNOW?

Derek appeared as himself in an episode of the popular sitcom *Seinfeld* and the Mark Wahlberg and Will Ferrell comedy movie *The Other Guys*.

Derek Jeter always dreamed of playing shortstop for the New York Yankees. He made that dream come true and more, becoming a five-time World Series champion, 14-time All-Star, Hall of Famer, World Series MVP, and one of the greatest players of all time. But how did he do it?

Well, very few dreams come true without support from others—Derek's support came from his parents. When he played Little League, he would look for his parents in the stands to feel more comfortable. Derek's parents encouraged him to follow his dreams, but they were also strict. The word "can't" wasn't allowed in their house, and they even made him sign a contract every year about how he could and couldn't behave. This wasn't easy for Derek, but he knew that his parents just wanted to help him achieve his dreams.

Derek became a great baseball player, but because he lived in Kalamazoo, Michigan, and not in a big city, people thought he couldn't make it to MLB. This motivated Derek! When people would tell him that no one from Kalamazoo would play shortstop for the Yankees, he'd respond, "Sorry you can't reach my dream, but I can, and I'm going to do everything in my power to prove you wrong."

Derek was good enough to be drafted as the sixth overall pick by the New York Yankees right out of high school, though they had him start with a minor-league team in Tampa Bay. Derek injured his ankle early on and wasn't playing well. He played so badly that some teammates wouldn't even talk to him. Derek

was so miserable, he often cried, thinking he'd made a terrible mistake, and wondering if he should have played college baseball instead.

In his second year, Derek was sent to a different minor league and things got worse. He made 56 errors that year—nearly one every other game! Derek missed so many balls that he lost confidence and didn't even want the ball to come his way anymore. Derek called his parents every night. Talking to them, Derek understood that this experience was a test of how committed he was to baseball. He believed that he would get better if he kept working hard.

In 1994, Derek's determination and hard work started to pay off. He even won Minor League Player of the Year! In 1995, Derek finally got called up to the Yankees. He wasn't always playing, but sitting on the bench and watching the team make the playoffs motivated him to have an incredible season in 1996. He won Rookie of the Year and helped lead the Yankees to a World Series victory.

Derek was successful with his unique inside-out hitting style, which became known as the Jeterian hit. He was also amazing at stealing bases, scoring runs, and throwing to get out other players. Between 1998 and 2000, Derek and the Yankees went on a legendary run, winning the World Series three years in a row.

In 2001, Derek would show how clutch he was. In the American League Division Series, Derek ran from his shortstop position to a spot in between first base and home, caught the ball off a bounce, and flipped it to home plate to get an out and save the Yankees from elimination. In Game 4 of the World Series, with the Yankees down 2-1 in the series, Derek hit a game-winning walk-off home run. Although the Yankees lost the series, Derek's playoff heroics earned him the "Mr. November" nickname, because this was the first playoff game ever in November.

In 2004, the Yankees signed another superstar—Alex Rodriguez. Alex also played shortstop, but the Yankees kept Derek at shortstop while Alex moved to third base. Derek would prove that he belonged at shortstop, making an epic play that season

called "The Dive." He ran toward the stands and dove into where the fans were sitting, catching the ball and getting the out.

Things seemed great for the Yankees as their superstar duo led them to a 3–0 lead in the American League Championship Series. They were just one game away from the World Series! But then the Yankees started playing like they were more focused on individual success instead of team success. For example, the team could have bunted more, hitting a soft hit to help a player on base get to the next one, even if it usually gets the batter out. But players didn't want to give up their chance to get a big hit. Although they were up 3–0, the Yankees lost the series in one of the biggest collapses in baseball playoff history.

Still, Derek continued working hard, staying consistent and leading the Yankees to wins—in the regular season. The Yankees and the man known as Mr. November didn't win a single playoff series between 2005 and 2007. In 2008, they didn't even make the playoffs! But in 2009, the Yankees finally learned to play as a team again. They won the 2009 World Series, making Derek a five-time champion.

In 2011, Derek became the all-time leader in games played for the Yankees. But after nearly 20 years of playing professional baseball, Derek was getting injured more often and playing less. Still, the length of his career allowed him to keep reaching new heights.

At age 40, Derek announced that the 2014 season would be his last. During his last season, Derek broke the all-time record for starts at shortstop and for this, and his many achievements as one of the best baseball players of all time, he became the 15th player to be given the Commissioner's Historic Achievement Award.

Derek's last season was a celebration of his amazing career. Even teams he'd beaten and fans who'd booed him came together to cheer him on and celebrate his career. Derek's final time batting in Yankee Stadium saw him hit a memorable single-run game-winning walk-off.

After his baseball career, Derek launched the Players' Tribune, a website for athletes to tell their own stories. He published a letter to his younger self on the site, saying, "If there is one key to success that I can give you, it's to treat every game like you're still in Little League. [. . .] If you can embrace that mindset even in the majors, then the last at bat won't exist. There's no failure. There is only the moment. The pitcher. The ball. The *game*. The thing that you love more than anything in the world. And the beauty of baseball is that every day is a new chance to get it right."

JOSÉ BAUTISTA

8

JOSÉ BAUTISTA

POSITION: Right fielder, third baseman

BIRTH DATE: October 19, 1980

HOMETOWN: Santo Domingo, Dominican Republic

TEAMS: Toronto Blue Jays, Baltimore Orioles, Tampa Bay Devil Rays, Kansas City Royals, Pittsburgh Pirates, Atlanta Braves, New York Mets, Philadelphia Phillies

BREAKOUT MOMENT: After struggling to find his place in MLB, in 2010 José led the league in home runs, becoming the 26th player to ever hit 50 home runs in a season.

TOP ACHIEVEMENTS

- Six-time All-Star
- Two-time MLB home run leader
- Three-time Silver Slugger Award winner
- Two-time Hank Aaron Award winner
- Toronto Blue Jays Level of Excellence
- Canadian Baseball Hall of Fame

DID YOU KNOW?

José is a huge soccer fan and primary owner of the United Soccer League team Las Vegas Lights FC.

Growing up in the Dominican Republic, José loved baseball. But his parents wanted him to focus on his education first. If he kept his grades up, he could play baseball. José worked hard, both on and off the baseball diamond. He learned to speak English and did well in math and science. Some of his friends started signing professional baseball contracts at 16 years old, but José knew it was important for him to finish school.

José continued his baseball training while taking business classes, in the hopes of getting a good offer from a professional baseball team. But he mostly got very low offers. He knew he wouldn't be able to make a career out of baseball with such a low salary.

José thought about giving up on his dream of playing baseball but decided not to. He kept working to get better, and his persistence paid off. José was drafted in the 20th round of the 2000 draft by the Pittsburgh Pirates. Still, education was so important to him that he later went back to school to earn his degree in business.

José spent four years in the minor leagues before getting called up to the Baltimore Orioles in 2004. Teams were having a hard time finding the good in him. That year alone, he played for the Tampa Bay Devil Rays, Kansas City Royals, New York Mets, and then returned to the Pirates. José became the first MLB player to appear on five different teams in one season. All these moves made him feel unsure about his future. Because he wasn't able to settle down in one place, José wasn't playing as well as he knew he could.

José stayed in Pittsburgh for four years. His career wasn't starting out well at all, but he did show that he could hit home runs and get RBIs. In 2008, he got traded to the Toronto Blue Jays, and this is where he would find his place in the league.

José's new hitting coach, Dwayne Murphy, saw how powerful of a hitter José was and helped him adjust his swing with a new technique. Dwayne taught José to increase his bat speed so he could maximize his power. With this new technique, José was able to start his swing early. This gave him more time to read the pitch and stop if it was a bad pitch, or hit with speed and power if it was a good one.

In 2010, at 29 years old, José was ready for his breakout season. He started slowly at first, but in May, he got 12 home runs and started regularly getting on base. That same month, he was recognized by MLB with his first Player of the Week award.

Before June was over, he already hit more home runs in the first half of the season than he'd hit in an entire season, with 24 of them. This made José an All-Star for the first time in his career!

José wasn't a one-hit wonder, though. In April 2011, he broke the Blue Jays' record for walks in a month and won Player of the Month. José couldn't stop hitting home runs.

In fact, he became the first player in over 70 years to hit the most home runs in the league for five straight months.

José couldn't find a spot on a team before, but now? He received the most All-Star votes in history and was invited to participate in MLB's Home Run Derby.

Because the Blue Jays are the only Canadian MLB team, José was easily one of the most popular baseball players in an entire country! He was on the cover of the 2012 and 2013 Canadian editions of *MLB The Show* video game.

José was an All-Star for the next four seasons, but in 2015, his popularity exploded with one of the most memorable playoff moments in baseball history.

In 1992 and 1993, the Blue Jays were on top of the baseball world, winning back-to-back World Series titles. But after that, they didn't make it back to the playoffs until 2015! Not only did José and the Blue Jays make the playoffs, but they won their division, and they scored 127 more runs than any other team that year.

In the American League Division Series, the Blue Jays were down two games in the

five-game series. Were they about to lose the first playoff series they had made in 22 years? They fought back to win the next two games.

In the seventh inning of the final game of the series, José, who was also known as "Joey Bats," was up at bat. The game was tied, 3–3, but the Blue Jays had runners on second and third base. José hit a massive three-run homer that looked like it was going to sail out of the ballpark. Caught up in the excitement and emotion, José flipped his bat high up in the air in an iconic moment known as "the bat flip." All the Blue Jays players rushed off the bench to celebrate. The Blue Jays won their first playoff series in nearly 25 years!

José had an entire country behind him, and for a fan base that had gone over 20 years without a championship, this moment felt like a championship. José will always be remembered for this moment—and for proving that it's never too late to find your way.

José didn't forget all the challenges he had to overcome early in his life. In 2011, he set up the Bautista Family Education Fund to help young amateur athletes from the Dominican Republic and Canada attend college, like he was able to do.

In 2023, José joined the Toronto Blue Jays Level of Excellence, where his name and number will stay forever. In 2025, José was inducted into the Canadian Baseball Hall of

Fame, where he reflected on his career, saying he succeeded because of “a lot of hard work and dedication. [. . .] There’s a lot of people and moments and hard-working hours in the batting cage that ultimately culminated with big-league success.”

2016 CHICAGO CUBS

9

2016 CHICAGO CUBS

TEAM STARS

Kris Bryant
third baseman

Theo Epstein
team president

Ben Zobrist
second baseman

Dexter Fowler
center fielder

Joe Maddon
manager

Javier Báez
shortstop/second and third baseman

Anthony Rizzo
first baseman

Addison Russell
shortstop

Jake Arrieta
pitcher

Jon Lester
pitcher

TOP ACHIEVEMENTS

- 2016 World Series champions
- Ended the longest World Series drought in MLB history

CLUTCH PLAYS

- In overtime in Game 7 of the World Series, Ben Zobrist and Miguel Montero drove in RBIs to put the Cubs up for good.
- Mostly unknown pitcher Mike Montgomery closed out the Cubs' final inning in Game 7 to win the World Series.

For a long time, people would joke about something unlikely happening by saying, "It'll happen when the Chicago Cubs win the World Series!" In 2016, it had been over 100 years since the Cubs last won the World Series in 1908. That was so long ago, sliced bread hadn't even been invented!

Legend has it that in 1945—the last time the Cubs were in the World Series—someone put a curse on the Cubs because their goat wasn't allowed into the stadium. It was called "the Curse of the Billy Goat." This may sound silly, but there were some shocking playoff moments that made the curse seem real!

In Game 6 of the 2003 National League Championship Series, outfielder Moisés Alou was about to catch a foul ball to get an important out that the Cubs would need to make it back to the World Series. But an overexcited Cubs fan reached over and stopped him from catching the ball. The next pitch was ball four, which meant the Florida Marlins' batter walked. This changed the momentum, and the Marlins came back to win 8-3.

Many believed the curse was real and would last forever, but that all started to change in 2011, when the Cubs hired Theo Epstein as team president. Epstein was president of the Boston Red Sox when they won the World Series in 2004 and famously broke their Curse of the Bambino from when they traded Babe Ruth in 1920. Clearly, Epstein had experience in helping teams break longtime curses!

Epstein built one of the best rosters in baseball, drafting players like shortstop Javier Báez, center fielder Albert Almora, third baseman/designated hitter Kris Bryant, and left fielder/designated hitter Kyle Schwarber. He also traded for players the Cubs believed they could develop, like first baseman Anthony Rizzo, shortstop Addison Russell, and center fielder Dexter Fowler. The Cubs also signed star free agent pitcher Jon Lester and added the final piece by signing Joe Maddon to be their new manager.

In 2016, the Cubs won their first two games, including a 9-0 opening day win. But in their third game, it looked like the curse was back. Fowler and Schwarber ran into each other trying to catch a fly ball, causing a season-ending injury for Schwarber. However, the Cubs bounced back, as Rizzo got six RBIs while Fowler got two RBIs to win the game.

From there, the Cubs dominated the regular season. They had the best record in the league with 103 wins, and seven Cubs players made the All-Star Game. In the postseason, they beat the San Francisco Giants in the National League Division Series and the Dodgers in the Championship Series. For the first time since 1945, they were back in the World Series, against the team that had gone the second-longest without winning: Cleveland, who hadn't won since 1948.

Cleveland started out strong, going up three games to one. It seemed like Chicago's curse was going to continue. But in Game 5, Jon Lester pitched a great game and their entire offense came together to help deliver the win. In Game 6, the team hit four home runs—two from Bryant, one from Russell, and one from Rizzo—to win and give them a chance to win it all.

Game 7 started strong for the Cubs, with Kyle Hendricks, who led the league in ERA, as their starting pitcher. Fowler and Báez both hit home runs. The Cubs were up 5-1 at the top of the fifth inning. In the bottom of the fifth inning, relief pitcher Lester came in, along with catcher David Ross. Ross and Lester had won a World Series together in 2013, and Ross was playing in his last game. Sounds like the start of an amazing sports fairy tale, doesn't it?

But what happened couldn't have been further from it. Lester threw a bad pitch that led to a hit, and Ross threw his ball off target, which led to two runners advancing. Next, Lester threw a pitch that bounced off the dirt into Ross's mask so hard that it knocked him back. While Ross recovered, Cleveland scored two runs. Ross wouldn't give up. He hit a home run to put the Cubs up 6–3!

But in the bottom of the eighth, relief pitcher Aroldis Chapman allowed a run and a two-run home run to tie the game at 6–6. The game went into extra innings. The Cubs were upset with themselves for losing their lead.

Suddenly, it started to rain so heavily they needed to call a 20-minute delay and bring tarps out to cover the field. But the Cubs would take advantage of this to hit the reset button.

DID YOU KNOW?

The Chicago Cubs were the first team to come back from being down three games to one in a World Series.

Former All-Star Jason Heyward called a players-only meeting during the delay, firing up his team for one last push. He said, "We're the best team in baseball. [. . .] Now we're going to show it. We play like the score is nothing-nothing. We've got to stay positive and fight for your brothers. Stick together and we're going to win this game."

Heyward's speech lifted the team's spirits, and they came back into the game convinced they could win. At the top of the 10th inning, the Cubs scored two runs. One of these runs was started by Schwarber, who hit a single. Because he had just returned from his knee

injury, Almora came in to run for Schwarber, showing the Cubs' teamwork. Almora ended up scoring a run off a hit from Ben Zobrist, and Rizzo scored a run off a hit from Miguel Montero. The Cubs were up 8–6!

When the Cubs were pitching again, they replaced Chapman with Carl Edwards Jr., who got two outs. But then Cleveland scored a run—they were catching up! Mike Montgomery came in to pitch. With one strike remaining,

he threw it to Cleveland's Michael Martinez, who hit a ground ball to third. Bryant ran up to grab it and threw to first to get Martinez out. The Cubs won their first World Series in over 100 years!

The 2016 Cubs proved that nothing bad lasts forever if you never give up. They came together as a team and believed in themselves to accomplish what once seemed impossible.

MOOKIE BETTS

10

MOOKIE BETTS

POSITION: Right fielder, shortstop, second baseman

BIRTH DATE: October 7, 1992

HOMETOWN: Nashville, Tennessee

TEAMS: Boston Red Sox, Los Angeles Dodgers

BREAKOUT MOMENT: In 2018, Mookie Betts became the first player in MLB history to win the World Series, MVP, Silver Slugger Award, Gold Glove Award, and the batting title in the same year.

TOP ACHIEVEMENTS

- Three-time World Series champion
- 2018 American League MVP
- 2018 American League batting champion
- Seven-time Silver Slugger Award winner
- Six-time Gold Glove Award winner

DID YOU KNOW?

Mookie is also a professional tenpin bowler and bowled a perfect game in the 2017 World Series of Bowling.

With three World Series wins, Mookie Betts has more championships than any current player, as of 2025. He's an MVP, batting champion, seven-time Silver Slugger Award winner, six-time Gold Glove Award winner, and three-time scoring leader. But did you know that most people thought Mookie was too short to ever be successful in baseball?

In fact, when he was a kid, he was so small that no Little League team wanted him! Mookie loved baseball as a kid, so this was hard for him, but his mom started her own team so Mookie could play. His mom's can-do attitude inspired Mookie to look for answers to his problems instead of giving up.

And guess what? Mookie was good! In his junior year of high school, he had an incredible .548 batting average while stealing 24 bases. He received a full scholarship offer to the University of Tennessee to play baseball, but he dreamed of playing in MLB. In 2010, while he was still in high school, Mookie went to the

East Coast Professional Showcase, which was attended by scouts from all 30 MLB teams.

Mookie was one of the smallest players there, and again, he was overlooked because of his size. Only one scout noticed him: Boston Red Sox area scout Danny Watkins. Watkins could tell how comfortable and confident Mookie looked on the field.

One play especially stuck out: Mookie was playing shortstop and effortlessly picked up a ball and threw it behind his back to second base. Watkins thought Mookie could be great at many positions—and he was right! Mookie would go on to play outfield, shortstop, and second base.

In the 2011 draft, Mookie was selected by the Red Sox in the fifth round as the 172nd pick. He started on their minor-league team but was struggling to hit the ball far. Mookie could have listened to the doubters who said he was too small to be a strong hitter. But he remembered how his mom refused to take no for an answer. Instead of focusing on the problem, Mookie got help and found a solution.

Working with a coach, Mookie discovered that if he removed a big leg kick from his swinging style, his timing would improve and he could hit the ball farther. By making this small change, he became one of the best players in the minor leagues.

In 2014, Mookie was called up to the Red Sox major-league team, but he struggled and had to go back to the minors. Mookie bounced between the minors and majors, but he never quit and always tried his best. Later that year, he earned an official spot with the Red Sox.

Mookie was finally able to showcase his skills. He was an excellent batter with a high batting average. Mookie also showed how his size could be an advantage. He was small but fast, so he was great at stealing bases. Mookie also proved that his size wouldn't hold him back from other parts of the game. He could jump incredibly high to catch balls in the outfield and take powerful swings despite his size.

Mookie was becoming a star! In 2016, he was an All-Star for the first time. In 2018, Mookie became the only player ever to lead the league in batting average *and* runs scored, and win the American League MVP, Silver Slugger Award, Gold Glove Award, and the World Series in the same season. But the Red Sox didn't want to pay Mookie what he was worth. They traded him to the Dodgers, where he signed a 12-year, $365 million extension.

In Mookie's first season with the Dodgers, he won another Gold Glove Award and

Silver Slugger Award and was named to All-MLB First Team for the first time. But Mookie would shine brightest in the National League Championship Series against the Atlanta Braves.

The Dodgers were down three games to one in the seven-game series. They had to win Game 5! The Dodgers were down 2-0, when Mookie ran faster than a speeding race car to catch a ball right before it hit the ground and had a perfect throw to home plate for a double play, getting two players out. This shifted the momentum in the Dodgers' favor, and they went on to win the game.

Mookie had an even bigger moment to win Game 6. National League home run leader Marcell Ozuna hit what looked like a two-run homer. Mookie leaped in the air like a superhero and caught the ball behind his head, letting out a burst of emotion and celebrating with his teammates.

But Mookie wasn't done yet. In Game 7, National League MVP Freddie Freeman hit what looked like a home run, but Mookie once again leaped up, leaning so far back he hit the outfield wall padding, and caught the ball. These three plays made Mookie a baseball legend—and helped the Dodgers get to the World Series. Mookie went on to win his second World Series title and was named *Sports Illustrated*'s 2020 Player of the Year.

In the next few seasons, Mookie played well, but the Dodgers couldn't seem to make it very far in the playoffs. The Dodgers decided to get Mookie more help. They signed arguably the best player in baseball: two-way pitching and batting superstar Shohei Ohtani.

The Dodgers' shortstop wasn't playing well, so they asked Mookie to "step up to the plate" and play shortstop for the first time since high school. Mookie knew it would be hard, but he took on the challenge. Mookie's willingness to do what the team needed paid off. The Dodgers made it back to the World Series in 2024—and won!

Mookie is almost always the smallest player on the field, but he never let what others thought define him. He became a champion by believing in himself even when others didn't. Mookie later reflected on how he would cheer himself on as a kid: "I think that energy and that effort that you put into cheering yourself on makes you feel better, and nobody's going to treat you better than you. [. . .] Be your own best friend."

AARON JUDGE

11

AARON JUDGE

POSITION: Right fielder

BIRTH DATE: April 26, 1992

HOMETOWN: Linden, California

TEAM: New York Yankees

BREAKOUT MOMENT: In 2017, Aaron won the American League Rookie of the Year Award after leading the American League in home runs with 52.

TOP ACHIEVEMENTS

- Seven-time All-Star
- Two-time American League MVP
- Two-time Hank Aaron Award winner
- Three-time American League home run leader
- 2023 Roberto Clemente Award winner
- 2017 American League Rookie of the Year

DID YOU KNOW?

Aaron was adopted by his parents, teachers Wayne and Patty Judge, the day after he was born. He still calls them every day.

Aaron Judge is one of the best and most popular players in baseball today. In less than 10 years in MLB, Aaron is already considered the best hitter of his generation and one of the best home run hitters of all time. But he had to overcome his public struggles on the baseball diamond early in his career to get there.

Aaron loved baseball from a young age, playing Little League as a kid. In high school, he branched out and played basketball, baseball, and football. He was so good at football that most colleges that recruited him wanted him to come play football for them!

Maybe it was because Aaron was six feet, seven inches tall, and they didn't think someone this tall could be a good baseball player. But Aaron wanted to play baseball, so he decided to go to Fresno State, a smaller school where they were going to let him play baseball.

From this point on, Aaron appeared destined for success. He had a .358 batting average and became an All-American

Freshman in his first year. He made All-Conference every year and won the 2012 College Home Run Derby.

Aaron was one of the best players in college, but teams still thought that his size just wouldn't work in the MLB. Every team passed on him in the first round, except for the Yankees. They took Aaron with the 32nd pick in the 2013 draft and sent him to play for their minor-league team.

Unfortunately, right before the season started, Aaron tore his quadriceps muscle in his leg. But he didn't sit and feel sorry for himself! He kept studying and watching film so he could improve as a player, even when he couldn't play. Once he returned, Aaron finished with an impressive batting average of .333 and hit nine home runs. But some scouts still questioned his consistency and whether he was too big to play.

On August 13, 2016, Aaron finally got called up from the minor leagues to play for the Yankees in MLB. Aaron hit a home run his first time batting! Things couldn't have gotten off to a better start! You might think it was smooth sailing for Aaron from this point on. But he was still getting used to MLB and finished the season with a low batting average of .179 and a very high strikeout rate of 42 percent.

Aaron used his bad start as motivation to get better. Even today, Aaron has a note in his phone that says .179. He looks at it to remind himself how far he's come and to keep trying hard.

Aaron would come very far, very quickly. In 2017, his first full season, he had one of the best rookie seasons of all time. He hit 52 home runs—the most ever for a rookie at the time—and became the first rookie to win the Home Run Derby. He also had 208 strikeouts, which was a lot, but just like Babe Ruth before him, Aaron knew that you've got to take big swings and be willing to fail to have success.

In 2022, Aaron did something no one thought was possible. He hit his 62nd home run, beating Roger Maris's American League record that had stood for over 60 years! He also led the league with 131 RBIs and secured a .311 batting average as he won his first American League MVP Award.

Aaron had become one of the superstars of the league, and the Yankees wanted him to be the face of their team. They signed him to a huge nine-year, $360 million contract. Aaron was on top of the world—and he was named team captain, too!

But in 2024, Aaron started the season in a slump. He had his lowest OPS—a measurement of a hitter's ability to get on base and hit for extra bases—of his career. He was batting less than .200. But Aaron stayed calm. He kept leading his teammates and worked with his coaches to get better.

As Aaron said, "You never know what's going to happen. But as long as I'm focused on keeping it simple—flush the bad days, don't sit too high on the good days . . . [I can] look back and be like, all right. I had a bad stretch here, I had a good stretch there. But right now? It's just even-keel."

Aaron knows that there is no success without the hard times. He broke out of his slump, hitting over 50 home runs that season. He's only the fifth player to do so in at least three seasons. He also led the league in RBIs and won the Hank Aaron Award, Silver Slugger Award, and his second American League MVP.

Aaron and the Yankees made it all the way to the World Series. But Aaron didn't perform his best, and they lost to Shohei Ohtani, Mookie Betts, and the Dodgers.

Losing the World Series was tough for Aaron, but he came back more determined than ever in 2025. He had the best start of his career yet, becoming the first player ever to score 5 home runs and 15 RBIs in the first six games of the season. He also started the season with a batting average over .400, one of the highest averages to start a season of all time. He even won the American League Player of the Month for the 11th time, breaking Alex Rodriguez's all-time record, and received the most votes to be selected as an All-Star.

In July 2025, Aaron became the fastest player to ever hit 350 career home runs! He appears to be on pace to break the all-time home run record.

Fans don't just love Aaron because he's an incredible baseball player. They love him because he's relatable, kind, and an excellent teammate and leader. He also founded the Aaron Judge ALL RISE Foundation to inspire kids to become responsible citizens. The foundation runs baseball camps and programs for children and donates money to other programs that help kids. For his positive impact on the community, Aaron was given the 2023 Roberto Clemente Award.

Aaron is still writing his baseball legacy. But if there's anything to know about him, it's that he will take this latest challenge of losing in the World Series and use it to fuel his success in the future.

SHOHEI OHTANI

12

SHOHEI OHTANI

POSITION: Pitcher, designated hitter

BIRTH DATE: July 5, 1994

HOMETOWN: Mizusawa (Ōshū), Iwate, Japan

TEAMS: Hokkaido Nippon-Ham Fighters, Los Angeles Angels, Los Angeles Dodgers

BREAKOUT MOMENT: In 2021, Shohei struck out 156 batters as a pitcher and hit 46 home runs, showing he was the best two-way player since Babe Ruth.

TOP ACHIEVEMENTS

- 2024 World Series champion
- Two-time American League MVP
- 2024 National League MVP
- Five-time All-Star
- Two-time home run leader
- Two-time Hank Aaron Award winner
- Commissioner's Historic Achievement Award

DID YOU KNOW?

Shohei's dog, Dekopin, popularly known as Decoy, is known as the Dodgers' "Most Valuable Pet."

Shohei Ohtani may be challenging Babe Ruth as baseball's greatest and most unique player of all time. Over 100 years after Babe started playing, Shohei—nicknamed "Shotime"—is the first player since Babe to rack up huge pitching *and* batting numbers. And he can steal bases like Jackie Robinson! He has multiple MVPs and a World Series title, but his journey may be even more impressive than his statistics.

Shohei was dedicated to making his baseball dreams come true. He even lived at his high school, under his coach's care, so he could focus on baseball! It wasn't easy for Shohei to be away from his family, but he would do anything to get better at baseball.

That included doing chores like cleaning toilets. His coach believed doing chores would help Shohei learn to be disciplined and humble. Shohei's hard work paid off. In 2012, he pitched the fastest fastball in Japanese high school history at the time, at 99 miles per hour.

Shohei wanted to play in MLB, but the American teams that recruited him only wanted him as a pitcher—including the Dodgers, his dream team. The Hokkaido Nippon-Ham Fighters in Japan's Nippon Professional Baseball were the only team willing to let him pitch *and* bat. Shohei chose to sign with them, so he could show that he could do both at a professional level.

This might have seemed like a step backward for some, but Shohei understood that you often have to take smaller steps to make a big dream come true. In fact, Shohei created a "dream board" to help him achieve his goals. He wrote down eight things he wanted to improve in his game. For each goal, he wrote down eight smaller goals to get there.

Shohei played for the Nippon-Ham Fighters for five years. In 2017, it was time for Shohei to live his dream and go to MLB. Many teams were interested in Shohei, but he chose the Los Angeles Angels, who believed in him as a two-way player.

At first, Shohei struggled to adjust to life in the US and MLB. Shohei had to use a translator to help him communicate and connect with his teammates and coaches. He had a tough spring training, but he was willing to make changes, even to his batting stance.

The Angels believed in Shohei, and that helped him settle in. By the start of the

2018 season, he was hitting home runs and striking out batters in ways no one had seen in decades. He joined Babe as the only players ever with 10 pitching appearances *and* 20 home runs in a season.

But in June 2018, Shohei injured his throwing arm. He could still hit, though—so well that he won the American League Rookie of the Year. After the season, Shohei had surgery. He struggled with his recovery and other injuries throughout 2019 and 2020. There were even times that Shohei thought about not trying to be a two-way player anymore. But he didn't give up, and the Angels didn't give up on him.

In 2021, Shohei was finally healthy, and he had one of the best seasons in baseball history. He hit 46 home runs with his powerful batting and struck out 156 hitters.

Shohei was awarded the Commissioner's Historic Achievement Award—the only player to receive the award in the past decade. Shohei was a superstar, and everyone was talking about him!

But Shohei also had his doubters. Some journalists said that Shohei couldn't be the face of the league, because he needed an interpreter to help him communicate in English. But Shohei proved that it's not what you look like or what language you speak, but who you are and how you make people feel that allows you to connect with others. In 2022, he became the first player in baseball's modern era to appear on both the hitting and pitching leaderboards in one season.

In 2023, Shohei and his Angels teammate Mike Trout were arguably the game's biggest stars. But the teammates were about to play against each other in the championship game of the World Baseball Classic. Shohei was Japan's captain, and Mike was Team USA's captain.

At the bottom of the ninth inning, Team USA already had two outs, and the game was on the line. Mike was at bat, and Shohei was pitching. Shohei threw a pitch as Mike swung and missed. Shohei struck out his own superstar teammate to win in one of the most-watched baseball games ever!

That same year, Shohei led the American League in home runs with 44 while recording 10 wins as a pitcher. He was named the American League MVP, becoming the only player to ever be unanimously voted MVP twice. But he wasn't done. In November 2023, he wrote down his next goal: World Champion.

Despite all his individual success, Shohei and the Angels never made the playoffs. But in December 2023, Shohei signed a 10-year, $700 million contract—the richest in sports history at the time—with the Dodgers, the team he dreamed of playing for as a kid. Unfortunately, Shohei suffered another injury and couldn't pitch. But with a combination of strength, speed, and smarts, Shohei became the first player ever to score 50 home runs and steal 50 bases, creating "the 50-50 club."

Shohei was once again named MVP, this time for the National League. And he took another step further: Shohei finally made the playoffs. He didn't disappoint, leading the Dodgers all the way to a World Series

championship! Shohei had written down his "World Champion" dream less than a year before, and now it had come true.

Shohei still has a lot of baseball left in him, but he's already thinking ahead. His next dream? To keep positively impacting others. As Shohei said, "Baseball has given me a purpose. It's become a way of life. [. . .] To be honest, I don't really know what kind of influence I have on other people, but I hope it's positive in some way. That would be reason enough to keep doing what I do right now."

Post-Game Notes

Can you believe you just read over 100 years of baseball stories spanning from the late 1800s to today? Baseball has been around seemingly forever, and the history of the sport represents our own history, the lessons we can learn, and the future we can have.

Players like Shohei Ohtani, Mookie Betts, and Jim Abbott taught us that you can have unique paths to success. Roberto Clemente, Hank Aaron, and Jackie Robinson and the 1947 Brooklyn Dodgers taught us the value of standing up for what's right and fighting for equal rights.

The 2016 Chicago Cubs and Reggie Jackson taught us to overcome the doubters by continuing to try no matter what. We learned how players who went on to become some of the greatest of their generation, like Derek Jeter and Aaron Judge, overcame struggles by continuing to work hard. Babe Ruth and José

Bautista showed us that you can overcome difficult starts to achieve greatness by never giving up.

As you reflect on these stories, ask yourself:

- Which story meant the most to me?
- How can I stay motivated, even if someone doubts me?
- What's something I believe is right to stand up for?
- What is my dream? What are some smaller steps I can take to make it come true?
- What's something I'm good at that can help me achieve my dream?

If you go after your dreams, never give up, and stay true to the lessons in this book, you can go from challenge to champion—and be a great person while doing it!

12 More Baseball Stars to Know

Here are 12 current players you can follow in MLB today!

RONALD ACUÑA JR. (RIGHT FIELDER)

At only 27 years old, Ronald Acuña Jr. is one of the best players in baseball. In 2018, Ronald was named National League Rookie of the Year after becoming the youngest player ever to hit five home runs and a grand slam in the playoffs. Ronald had a strong start in 2021 but got hurt halfway through the season, so all he could do was watch as his team, the Atlanta Braves, won the World Series. He had his best season yet in 2023, becoming the first

MLB player ever to steal at least 70 bases and hit 40 home runs, earning him the National League MVP. Sadly, injury struck again in 2024. But in 2025, Ronald hit a home run his first time batting and was selected as an All-Star. That's surely a sign of more good things to come!

ELLY DE LA CRUZ (SHORTSTOP)

Elly De La Cruz dreamed of playing in MLB as a kid. But to play in better tournaments and train in a better facility, he had to move away from his family. This decision would pay off: The Cincinnati Reds signed him when he was just 16 years old.

Elly is as tall as an NBA player, as fast as an Olympic runner, and as strong as an NFL player, making him one of baseball's most unique players! In 2024, he made his first All-Star Game while breaking records. Elly became the fifth player in history to hit at least 25 home runs and steal at least 65 bases—and the youngest to ever do it. In 2025, he made his second All-Star Game!

FREDDIE FREEMAN (FIRST BASEMAN)

Freddie Freeman, at 35 years old, is still one of baseball's best players. While 35 may be young in life, this is considered older for a baseball player. Freddie has faced injuries throughout his career, but in 2024, he would face his greatest challenge yet. During the season, his son came down with a rare and serious illness called Guillain-Barré syndrome. Freddie left the team to be with his son.

Once his son was getting better, Freddie returned to the team. He wasn't playing as well and sprained his ankle toward the end of the season. But, in Game 1 of the World Series, he hit a walk-off grand slam—one of the greatest plays in World Series history! The Dodgers won, and Freddie was named MVP.

VLADIMIR GUERRERO JR. (FIRST BASEMAN)

One of Vladimir Guerrero Jr.'s strongest memories is standing on the baseball field with his Hall of Fame dad, who was playing his last game for the Montreal Expos. Vladimir was just four years old, and 16 years later, he played his first major-league season with the Toronto Blue Jays.

In 2021, he led the league with 48 home runs, 123 runs scored, and 363 total bases, and became the youngest player ever to win All-Star MVP. He's been an All-Star every year since and was named to the All-MLB First Team for the second time in 2024. Vladimir is sure to be one of MLB's brightest stars for years to come.

GUNNAR HENDERSON (SHORTSTOP)

Gunnar Henderson is one of the best young players in MLB today, but he didn't get there alone. When Gunnar was a kid, his dad built a baseball field in their backyard so that he could practice. He was drafted by the Baltimore Orioles, but his first season in the minor leagues didn't go very well. But Gunnar kept working hard, and by 2022, Gunnar had gotten so good he was representing the Orioles at the All-Star Futures Game!

Finally, in 2023, Gunnar played his first full season for the Orioles in MLB. He didn't disappoint, hitting 28 home runs and 82 RBIs, and winning the American League Rookie of the Year Award in 2023. In 2024, he earned his first All-Star selection. Going into the 2025 season, Gunnar was ranked the 10th best player in MLB, at only 23 years old!

FRANCISCO LINDOR (SHORTSTOP)

Francisco Lindor's nickname is "Mr. Smile" because he always has a good attitude and loves playing baseball. In 2016, while playing for Cleveland, Francisco earned his first All-Star selection, won a Gold Glove Award, and became the first player under 23 years old with seven multi-hit games. He even helped lead Cleveland to a World Series appearance!

But when Francisco struggled in 2020, Cleveland traded him to the Mets. After a tough season in 2021, Francisco has gotten better every year, becoming one of three players ever with multiple seasons of 30 home runs and 25 stolen bases. In 2025, he joined Derek Jeter as one of three shortstops to have 200 home runs and 200 stolen bases. That same year, Francisco earned his first All-Star selection in six years!

CAL RALEIGH (CATCHER)

Seattle Mariners catcher Cal Raleigh proves it's never too late to have a breakout season. It took until he was 28 years old for people to recognize he was one of baseball's best players!

He may have started his career with plenty of doubters after some bad seasons, but in 2024, he would prove them wrong as he won the Gold Glove Award as the best catcher in baseball. In 2025, he would get off to the best start ever by a catcher. Catchers aren't known for hitting a lot of home runs, but that season, Cal became the first catcher to ever hit more than 30 home runs—38 to be exact—before the All-Star Game in July. Cal even became the first catcher to win the Home Run Derby! He has gone from being unknown to one of the most exciting players in baseball.

COREY SEAGER (SHORTSTOP)

Corey Seager is one of only four players in MLB history to win two World Series MVP Awards. In fact, he is the first player to win the World Series MVP in both the American League and National League! But he faced huge challenges to get there. In his first season with the Dodgers, Corey was National League Rookie of the Year and made the All-Star Game. But in 2018, injury struck and he was out for nearly the entire season. Corey came back, only to suffer another injury in 2019.

Then the COVID-19 pandemic happened in 2020. COVID rules meant Corey couldn't go into the video room to watch his swing after every play, something he was used to doing. Corey had to learn to swing based on his instincts. It worked! Corey led the Dodgers to a World Series title in 2020 and was named MVP, then won another title and MVP with the Texas Rangers in 2023.

PAUL SKENES (PITCHER)

Pittsburgh Pirates pitcher Paul Skenes is one of the best pitchers in baseball—and one of its most popular players. Paul was a baseball star from the time he helped LSU win the National College Championship in 2023, becoming an even bigger star after being selected first in the 2023 draft. But it's been tough for Paul to find time for himself while having people always wanting to take his picture and talk to him because he's so famous.

How does he stay ready for baseball with all the chaos? Paul uses meditation and his workout routine to stay focused and prepared, and it works! In 2024, he became the fifth rookie pitcher to ever be an All-Star. He ended his rookie season with an outstanding 1.96 ERA, 170 strikeouts, an 11–3 record, and was named the National League Rookie of the Year. In 2025, Paul was once again named an All-Star.

JUAN SOTO (RIGHT FIELDER)

Juan Soto is one of the best players in MLB, but did you know that as a kid, he had to play indoors because he lived in a rough neighborhood and that his dad helped him practice batting by pitching him bottle caps? Juan was just 21 when he helped lead the Washington Nationals to a World Series win and became one of the youngest players ever to win the Babe Ruth Award.

Juan is known for his signature "Soto Shuffle"—which looks like a dance move—when resetting his batting stance. In 2024, Soto helped the New York Yankees reach the World Series. Although they didn't win, Soto's play earned him the largest sports contract in history: $765 million over 15 years with the New York Mets. The Soto Shuffle will be dominating baseball for years to come!

MIKE TROUT (RIGHT FIELDER)

Los Angeles Angel Mike Trout is arguably the best baseball player of his generation. He can truly do it all! He is incredibly consistent at bat, batting over .300 for most of his career and hitting a ton of home runs. Growing up, Mike always wanted to be hitting a ball. He has joked that he feels bad because he was always asking his dad if he could go hit balls!

Mike is also consistent on defense, using his speed to get any ball coming his way. He can get on base and steal bases, too! He's an

11-time All-Star, nine-time Silver Slugger Award winner, and a three-time American League MVP.

But his biggest challenge? He's made the playoffs only once. Injuries have been hard on Mike, but as one of the greatest players of all time, he will continue to work hard and prove he can still play well. And off the field, now *he's* the dad whose son tells him he always wants to hit! It looks like the Trout legacy will live on for years to come.

BOBBY WITT JR. (SHORTSTOP)

Bobby Witt Jr. may be baseball's most exciting young player, but did you know he struggled with his confidence and was shy as a kid? He didn't even like people watching him play baseball! Today, he's the first shortstop in MLB history with two 30-30 seasons—that's 30 home runs and 30 stolen bases. Bobby can run the bases fast, steal bases, and sprint to make athletic catches, *and* he can hit powerful home runs.

Bobby's also known as a great teammate in the Kansas City Royals' dugout, always smiling and providing entertaining celebrations, even flapping his arms like a bird after scoring a home run. In 2024, he became an All-Star, won a Silver Slugger Award, a Gold Glove Award, and made the All-MLB First Team. In 2025, Bobby made the All-Star Game. And he did all this by 25!

Acknowledgments

As you've seen in this book, no dreams come true without the support of others, and I have some wonderful people to thank who helped make my dream of writing this book come true.

The first person I have to thank is Nonna, because whenever I think of baseball or see a Toronto Blue Jays logo, I will always think of her, and so will everyone who knew her. She was not only an enthusiastic sports fan who helped inspire my love of sports but also an avid reader and a great writer, too. She helped me understand how to write kids' books because watching kids' shows with her and seeing her love for them inspired me to always keep in touch with my own inner child. I'm so fortunate that she lived with my family growing up, to have experienced her love, and to know she's smiling down reading this now.

I also want to thank my mom, who had a unique career as both a journalist and human rights lawyer, and my dad, who had an amazing career in business, for inspiring me to pursue my dreams. Nonna was my mom's mom, and seeing the care my mom showed for her inspired me to be a caring person, too. Some of the people in this book are lucky to have encouraging, supportive parents, and I am, too.

I also want to thank everyone at Zeitgeist Publishing and Penguin Random House who made this book possible, including Ada Fung, Tahra Seplowin, Patty Consolazio, Erica Ferguson, Katy Brown, Portia Turner, Ariel Keith, Dan Janeck, and this book's illustrator, Lorenzo Fornaciari.

About the Author

Skyler Trepel is a multimedia sports and entertainment journalist and author from Winnipeg, Manitoba, Canada. Skyler has his bachelor of commerce with honors from the University of Manitoba, his film production diploma from the Toronto Film School, and his master of arts in specialized journalism from the University of Southern California.

Formerly a financial advisor, Skyler left that career to pursue his passion for sports and entertainment journalism and writing. He has written hundreds of articles for various publications and is currently a contributing sports and entertainment writer for *People* magazine/People.com and *Entertainment Weekly*. When not writing, Skyler loves spending time with his family, watching and playing sports, cooking, going to concerts, traveling, reading, spending time with friends, playing video games, watching TV and movies, and hanging out with his cat, Simba.

About the Illustrator

Lorenzo Fornaciari is an illustrator, graphic designer, and teacher. He has loved drawing his whole life, and after attending Scuola Internazionale di Comics in Reggio Emilia, Italy, he began work as a freelance illustrator. He has lived in the UK and Italy while creating illustrations for children's books, and was a teacher of storyboarding and Photoshop at Scuola Internazionale di Comics. He has worked on many exciting projects, from video games and animation to websites, comics, and board games.

Hi, parents and caregivers,

We hope your child enjoyed *Inspiring Stories of Baseball Greats*. If you have any questions or concerns about this book, or have received a damaged copy, please contact customerservice@penguinrandomhouse.com. We're here and happy to help.

Also, please consider writing a review on your favorite retailer's website to let others know what you and your child thought of the book!

Sincerely,

The Zeitgeist Team

SCORE THE REST OF THE BOOKS IN THE

SERIES!

"From overcoming challenges to advocating for change, *From Challenge to Champion* shows how true champions inspire us both on and off the field."

—ALLYSON FELIX, seven-time Olympic gold medalist and founder of Saysh

Stories of top athletes like Simone Biles, Serena Williams, Tom Brady, LeBron James, and others highlight the power of hard work and perseverance.

Featuring NFL stars like Saquon Barkley, Josh Allen, and Jerry Rice, read about the challenges these athletes have overcome on their path to triumph.

Alex Morgan. Lionel Messi. Marta. Vini Jr. What do they share? Resilience and the drive to win! Read about these top soccer players and more in this book.

Parents and caregivers can learn more about these books and upcoming titles at **zeitgeistpublishing.com**